Working Dogs

Contents **Page**

written by Pam Holden

Pet dogs have a job to do. They look after their home, and bark to say if someone comes. A good guard dog could even save its owners from a fire.

pets

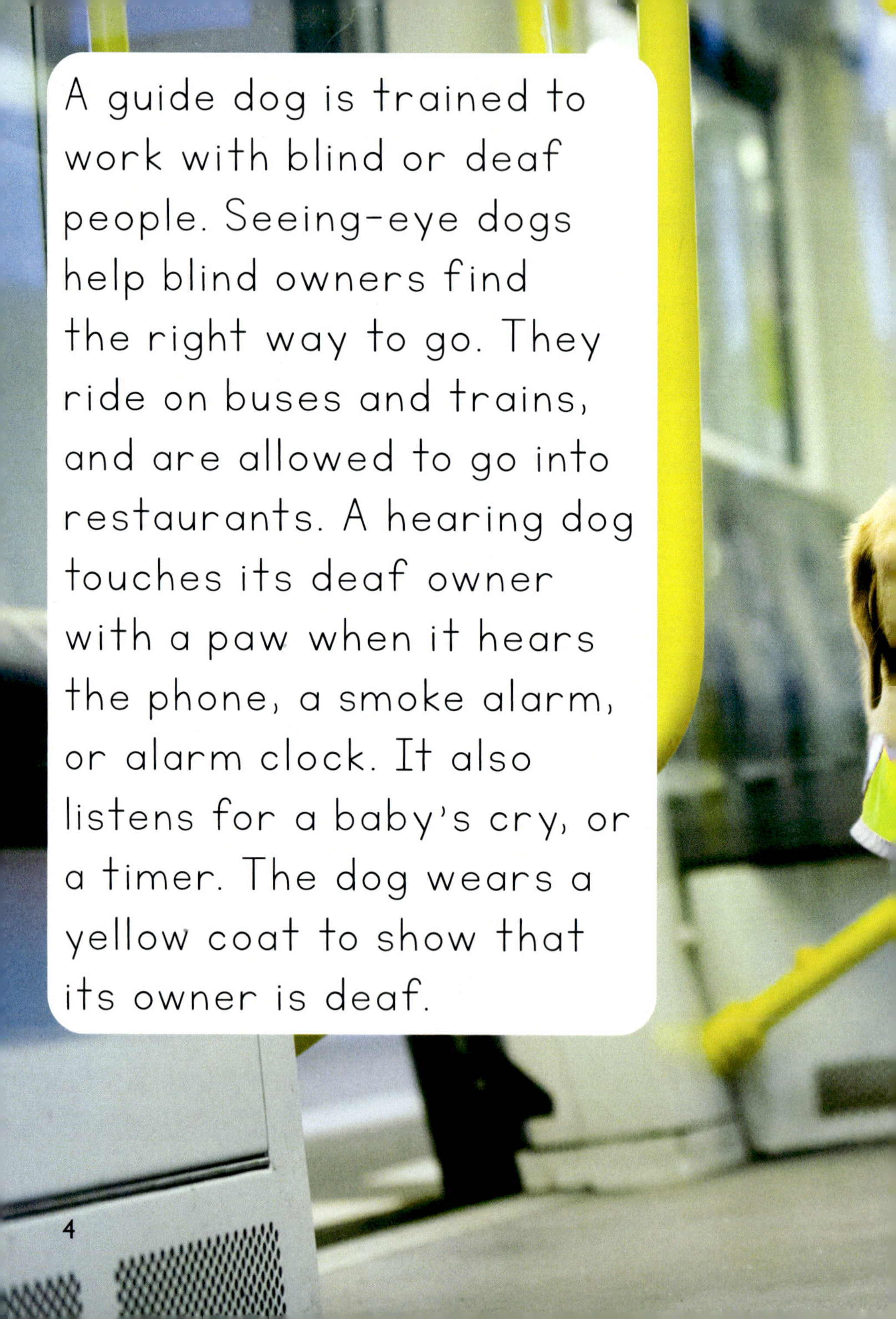

A guide dog is trained to work with blind or deaf people. Seeing-eye dogs help blind owners find the right way to go. They ride on buses and trains, and are allowed to go into restaurants. A hearing dog touches its deaf owner with a paw when it hears the phone, a smoke alarm, or alarm clock. It also listens for a baby's cry, or a timer. The dog wears a yellow coat to show that its owner is deaf.

guide dog

On farms, dogs help round-up sheep and cows by barking to move them.

Farmers whistle to give commands. These dogs are fast, can climb hills, and are clever at finding lost animals.

In very cold places, strong dogs pull sleds over ice and snow, carrying people or loads.

They wear a harness and work in teams. They must be smart, well-trained dogs, and respond to voice commands.

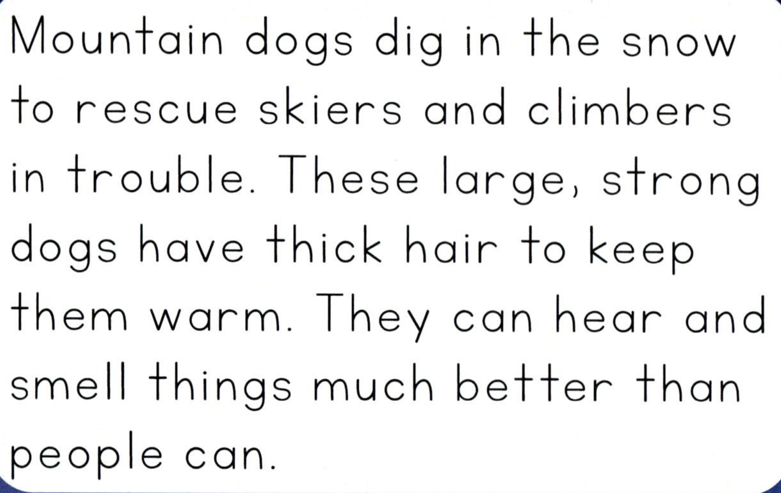

Mountain dogs dig in the snow to rescue skiers and climbers in trouble. These large, strong dogs have thick hair to keep them warm. They can hear and smell things much better than people can.

Police dogs are trained to help police find people who are hiding, or who run away.

These dogs are trained to jump over fences and walls as they follow a trail. Police dogs work to find things that have been stolen or hidden.

Tracker dogs are trained to find people who are lost. These dogs search until they sniff the missing people's smell on the ground or in the air. They lead rescuers to the missing people.

companions

Some dogs' job is to keep people company and make them smile!